Essential

mystic

Prayers

PARACLETE PRESS

PARACLETE PRESS
BREWSTER, MASSACHUSETTS

2018 First Printing

Essential Mystic Prayers

Copyright © 2018 by Paraclete Press, Inc.

ISBN 978-1-64060-066-9

The Paraclete Press name and logo (dove on cross) are trademarks of Paraclete Press, Inc.

Library of Congress Cataloging-in-Publication Data
Names: Paraclete Press.
Title: Essential mystic prayers.
Description: Brewster, MA : Paraclete Press, Inc., 2017.
Identifiers: LCCN 2017058688 | ISBN 9781640600669 (trade paper)
Subjects: LCSH: Prayers. | Mysticism. | Spiritual life.
Classification: LCC BL560 .E87 2017 | DDC 242/.8—dc23
LC record available at https://lccn.loc.gov/2017058688

10 9 8 7 6 5 4 3 2 1

All rights reserved. No portion of this book may be reproduced, stored in an electronic
retrieval system, or transmitted in any form or by any means—electronic, mechanical,
photocopy, recording, or any other—except for brief quotations in printed reviews, without
the prior permission of the publisher.

Published by Paraclete Press
Brewster, Massachusetts
www.paracletepress.com

Printed in the United States of America

Contents

God's Will

Suffering

Union with God

Holy Presence

Introduction

For the purposes of this little book, let us agree that the meaning of mysticism cannot be understood apart from the thoughts and voices and prayers of real people. And this book, as you will see, is filled with the mystical prayers of people who have been transformed by the Christian tradition. Throughout the history of Christianity (and, for that matter, through the history of most faiths), there have been women and men whose intense, direct experience of God has inspired them to share it in some way with others. They have spoken, sung, written, and sometimes even painted their experiences of God's presence, even when (*especially* when) that presence defied the ability of any kind of language to describe it. Whether we doubt, wonder about, fully accept, and or even aspire to such experiences, we can agree that these people came to know something about God that was unknowable any other way. And because they found a way to express it, we know something more about God as well.

These prayers give voice to those deep and enduring desires to know God that stir within hearts of faith. There are no "professional" mystics. These authors are poets, pastors, social workers, caretakers of the poor and the sick, husbands, wives, monks, nuns, theologians, scientists, teachers, pot scrubbers, and philosophers. In other words, they all had other work to do besides pray. And even if the authors may not be strictly identified with the mystical tradition, their prayers still reflect those qualities of longing for a sense of presence, of love for, and even union with God, that has been passed down through generations of those whom we have called "Christian mystics."

1

The prayer preceding all prayers is:
May it be the real I who speaks.
May it be the real Thou that I speak to.

—*C.S. Lewis*

Praise
&Trust

2

O burning Mountain,

O chosen Sun,

O perfect Moon,

O fathomless Well,

O unattainable Height,

O Clearness beyond measure,

O Wisdom without end,

O Mercy without limit,

O Strength beyond resistance,

O Crown beyond all majesty:

the humblest thing you created sings your praise.

—*Mechthild of Magdeburg*

3

We were created for you by yourself,
and towards you our face is set.
We acknowledge you,
our maker and creator;
we adore your wisdom and pray
that it may order all our life.
We adore your goodness and mercy, and
beg them ever to sustain and help us.

—*William of St-Thierry*

4

My God and my all!

—*Francis of Assisi*

Essential Mystic Prayers

5

Blessed be thy holy Name,
O Lord, my God!
For ever blessed be thy holy Name,
For that I am made
The work of thy hands,
Curiously wrought
By thy Divine Wisdom,
Enriched
By thy Goodness,
Being more thine
Than I am mine own.
O Lord!

—*Thomas Traherne*

6

You, O eternal Trinity,
are a deep sea into which,
the more I enter,
the more I find.
And the more I find,
the more I seek.
O abyss, O eternal Godhead,
O sea profound,
what more could you give me than yourself?
Amen.

—Catherine of Siena

7

Let nothing disturb you,
Let nothing frighten you,
All things are passing;
God only is changeless.
Patience gains all things.
Who has God wants nothing.
God alone suffices.

—*Teresa of Avila*

8

You, my God,
are love who loves,
and love who is lovable,
and love who is the bond between these two.

—*Nicholas of Cusa*

9

To lift up the hands in prayer gives God glory,
but a man with a dungfork in his hand,
a woman with a slop pail,
give Him glory, too.
God is so great that all things give Him glory
if you mean that they should.

—*Gerard Manley Hopkins*

10

O Christ, our Morning Star,
Splendor of Light Eternal,
shining with the glory of the rainbow,
come and waken us
from the greyness of our apathy,
and renew in us your gift of hope.
Amen.

—*Venerable Bede*

11

Come, my Light, and illumine my darkness.
Come, my Life, and revive me from death.
Come, my Physician, and heal my wounds.
Come, Flame of divine love,

and burn up the thorns of my sins,
kindling my heart with the flame
of thy love.

Come, my King,

sit upon the throne of my heart
and reign there.

For you alone are my King and my Lord.

—*Dimitrii of Rostov*

12

Lord God,
glory be to you eternally.
Amen.

—*Meister Eckhart*

13

Holy Spirit,
giving life to all life, moving all creatures,
root of all things, washing them clean,
wiping out their mistakes, healing their wounds,
you are our true life,
luminous, wonderful,
awakening the heart from its ancient sleep.

—*Hildegard of Bingen*

14

As soon as you come in the presence of God,
remain in respectful silence for a little while....
Simply Enjoy God.

—*Madame Guyon*

15

Christ be with me, Christ within me
Christ behind me, Christ before me
Christ beside me, Christ to win me
Christ to comfort me and restore me.
Christ beneath me, Christ above me
Christ in quiet, Christ in danger
Christ in hearts of all that love me
Christ in mouth of friend or stranger.

—*Patrick of Ireland*

All
to God

16

In you, Father all-mighty, we have our preservation and our
     bliss.

In you, Christ, we have our restoring and our saving.

You are our mother, brother, and savior.

In you, our Lord the Holy Spirit, is marvelous and plenteous
     grace.

You are our clothing; for love you wrap us and embrace us.

You are our maker, our lover, our keeper.

Teach us to believe that by your grace all shall be well,

and all shall be well,

and all manner of things shall be well. Amen.

—Julian of Norwich

17

Grant me, O Lord my God,
a mind to know you,
a heart to seek you,
wisdom to find you,
conduct pleasing to you,
faithful perseverance in waiting for you,
and a hope of finally embracing you.
Amen.

—*Thomas Aquinas*

Essential Mystic Prayers

18

Bring us, O Lord God, at our last awakening,
into the house and gate of heaven,
to enter into that gate and dwell in that house,
where there shall be no darkness nor dazzling,
but one equal light;
no noise nor silence but one equal music;
no fears nor hopes but one equal possession;
no ends nor beginnings but one equal eternity;
in the habitations of thy Majesty and thy Glory,
world without end. Amen.

—John Donne

19

Let Him easter in us,
be a dayspring to the dimness of us,
be a crimson-cresseted east.

—*Gerard Manley Hopkins*

20

Ever-faithful God, the house of my soul is too small for you
    to enter:
Make it more spacious by your coming.
It lies in ruins: rebuild it.

—*Augustine of Hippo*

Essential Mystic Prayers

21

O my God!

I offer you all my actions this day

for the intentions and for the glory of the Sacred Heart of
    Jesus.

I desire to sanctify every beat of my heart,

my every thought,

my simplest works,

by uniting them to his infinite merits;

and I wish to make reparation for my sins

by casting them into the furnace of his merciful love.

O my God!

I ask you for myself and for those whom I hold dear,

the grace to fulfill perfectly your holy will,

to accept for love of you the joys and sorrows of this passing
    life,

so that we may one day be united together in heaven for all
    eternity.

Amen.

—*Thérèse of Lisieux*

22

May all I do today begin with you, O Lord.
> Plant dreams and hopes within my soul,
> revive my tired spirit:
> be with me today.

May all I do today continue with your help, O Lord.
> Be at my side and walk with me:
> Be my support today.

May all I do today reach far and wide, O Lord.
> My thoughts, my work, my life:
> make them blessings for your kingdom;
> let them go beyond today,

O God, today is new, unlike any other day,
> for God makes each day different.
> Today God's everyday grace falls on my soul like
> abundant seed,
> though I may hardly see it....

—*John Henry Newman*

23

Take, Lord, and receive all my liberty,
my memory, my understanding,
and my entire will,
all I have and call my own.
You have given all to me.
To you, Lord, I return it.
Everything is yours; do with it what you will.
Give me only your love and your grace.
That is enough for me.

—*Ignatius of Loyola*

24

Lord, I glorify you in everything that happens to me.
In whatever manner you make me live and die, I am content.
Events please me for their own sake, regardless of their

    consequences,
because your action lies behind them.
Everything is heaven to me,
because all my moments manifest your love.

—*Jean-Pierre de Caussade*

Mercy & Peace

25

Lord Jesus Christ, Son of God, have mercy on me, a sinner.

—*The Jesus Prayer*

26

The words of the Our Father are perfectly pure.
If you recite the Our Father with no other intention
than to pay the fullness of one's attention on the words
    themselves,
you are completely sure to be delivered by this means from
    a part,
as small as it may be,
of the evil you hold inside you.

—*Simone Weil*

27

O blessed Jesus, give me stillness of soul in you.
Let your mighty calmness reign in me.
Rule me, O King of Gentleness,
King of Peace.

—*John of the Cross*

28

O my God,
you see how easily I lose heart
at the thought of my imperfections.
Nevertheless, I shall continue to strive for virtue.
Gladly will I forego all consolation
in order to offer you the fruit of my efforts.
I wish to make profit out of the smallest actions
and do them for love.

—*Thérèse of Lisieux*

Essential Mystic Prayers

29

King of Glory, King of Peace,
 I will love thee;
And that love may never cease,
 I will move thee.

Thou hast granted my request,
 Thou hast heard me:
Thou didst note my working breast,
 Thou hast spar'd me.

Wherefore with my utmost art
 I will sing thee,
And the cream of all my heart
 I will bring thee.

—*George Herbert*

30

My spirit has become dry because it forgets to feed on you.

—*John of the Cross*

31

Lord, I ask for your mercy.
Chastise me for my sins and purge me of all evil,
that I may be saved from everlasting damnation.
I am willing, even happy, to endure any suffering here on
      Earth,
that I may be spared the torments of hell.

—*Margery Kempe*

32

Lord, from you flows true and continual kindness.
You had cast us off and justly so,
but in your mercy you forgave us.
You were at odds with us,
and you reconciled us.
You had set a curse on us,
and you blessed us.
You had banished us from the garden,
and you called us back again.
You took away the fig leaves
that had been an unsuitable garment,
and you clothed us in a cloak of great value.
You flung wide the prison gates,
and you gave the condemned a pardon.
You sprinkled clean water on us,
and you washed away the dirt.

—*Gregory of Nyssa*

33

Look upon us, O Lord,
and let all the darkness of our souls
vanish before the beams of thy brightness.
Fill us with holy love,
and open to us the treasures of thy wisdom.
All our desire is known unto thee.
Therefore, perfect what thou hast begun,
and what thy Spirit has awakened us to ask in prayer.
We seek thy face;
turn thy face unto us, and show us thy glory.
Then shall our longing be satisfied,
and our peace shall be perfect.

—Augustine of Hippo

34

Let your goodness, Lord, appear to us, that we,
made in your image, conform ourselves to it.
In our own strength
we cannot imitate your majesty, power, and wonder,
nor is it fitting for us to try.
But your mercy reaches from the heavens
through the clouds to the earth below.
You have come to us as a small child,
but you have brought us the greatest of all gifts,
the gift of eternal love.
Caress us with your tiny hands,
embrace us with your tiny arms
and pierce our hearts with your soft, sweet cries.

—*Bernard of Clairvaux*

35

Tread out in my heart the path of repentance,
my God and my Lord, my hope and my boast,
my strong refuge, by whom may my eyes be illumined;
and may I have understanding of your truth, O Lord.

—*Isaac the Syrian*

36

Breath of life,
You ride the waves of life with me
in the rhythms of my communion with you.
You enter the comings and goings
of each day and in every prayer I breathe.
Whether I am in the stillness of quiet prayer
or in the fullness of the day's activity,
may your peace flow through my being.

—*Joyce Rupp*

37

O Lord and Master of my life,
grant me not a spirit of sloth, meddling,
love of power,
and idle talk.
But give to me, your servant, a spirit of sober-mindedness,
humility, patience,
and love.
Yes, O Lord and King,
grant me to see my own faults and not to judge my brother,
since you are blessed to the ages of ages.
Amen.

—*Ephrem the Syrian*

Wisdom
& Guidance

38

Thank you, Jesus, for bringing me this far.
In your light, I see the light of my life.
Your teaching is brief and to the point;
you persuade us to trust in God;
you command us to love one another.
You promise everything to those who obey your teaching;
you ask nothing too hard for a believer,
nothing a lover can refuse.
Your promises to your disciples are true, nothing but the
    truth.
Even more, you promise us yourself,
the perfection of all that can be made perfect.

—*Nicholas of Cusa*

39

I am not attempting, O Lord, to penetrate your loftiness,
for I cannot begin to match my understanding with it,
but I desire in some measure to understand your truth,
which my heart believes and loves.
For I do not seek to understand in order that I may believe,
but I believe in order to understand.
For this too I believe,
that "unless I believe, I shall not understand." (Isaiah 7:9)

—Anselm of Canterbury

40

My Lord God, I have no idea where I am going.
I do not see the road ahead of me.
I cannot know for certain where it will end,
nor do I really know myself,
and the fact that I think that I am following your will
does not mean that I am actually doing so.
But I believe that the desire to please you does in fact please
     you.
And I hope I have that desire in all that I am doing.
I hope that I will never do anything apart from that desire.
And I know that if I do this you will lead me by the right
     road,
though I may know nothing about it.
Therefore will I trust you always,
though I may seem to be lost and in the shadow of death.
I will not fear, for you are ever with me,
and you will never leave me to face my perils alone.

—*Thomas Merton*

41

All the while, Lord, as I pondered these things,
you stood by me;
I sighed and you heard me;
I was tossed to and fro and you steered me aright.
I wandered down the wide road of the world, but you did
not desert me.

—Augustine of Hippo

42

High and Holy God,
give me this day a word of truth
to silence the lies that would devour my soul
and kind encouragements
to strengthen me when I fall.
Gracious One, I come quietly to your door
needing to receive from your hands
the nourishment that gives life.
Amen and Amen.

—Bernard of Clairvaux

Essential Mystic Prayers

43

O Christ, the fulfillment of the truth,
let your truth rise in our hearts
and let us know how to walk in your way
according to your will.

—*Isaac the Syrian*

44

Grant me grace, O Lord my God,
that I may not falter in times of prosperity or adversity.
May I not be unduly lifted up by the first,
nor unduly cast down by the second.

—*Thomas Aquinas*

God's
Will

45

Give me, O Lord, I beseech you, courage to pray
for light and to endure the light here,
where I am on this world of yours,
which should reflect your beauty but which we
have spoiled and exploited.
Cast your radiance on the dark places,
those crimes and stupidities I like to ignore and gloss over.
Show up my pretensions, my poor little claims and
achievements, my childish assumptions of importance,
my mock heroism.
Take me out of the confused half-light in which I live.
Enter and irradiate every situation and every relationship.
Show me my opportunities, the raw material of love,
of sacrifice, of holiness, lying at my feet,
disguised under homely appearance
and only seen as it truly is, in your light.

—Evelyn Underhill

46

All Highest and Glorious God,
cast your light into the darkness of my heart.
Grant me right faith, firm hope, perfect charity,
profound humility,
with wisdom and perception, O Lord,
so that I may always and everywhere
seek to know and do what is truly your holy will,
through Jesus Christ our Lord. Amen.

—*Francis of Assisi*

47

Lord of all pots and pans and things,
since I've no time to be a great saint
by doing lovely things,
or watching late with Thee,
or dreaming in the dawn light,
or storming heaven's gates,
make me a saint by getting meals,
and washing up the plates.
Warm all the kitchen with Thy love,
and light it with Thy peace;
forgive me all my worrying,
and make my grumbling cease.
Thou who didst love to give men food,
in room, or by the sea,
accept the service that I do:
I do it unto Thee. Amen.

—*Brother Lawrence*

48

Dearest Jesus,
teach me to be generous,
to love and serve you as you deserve;
to give and not to count the cost,
to fight and not to heed the wounds,
to toil and not to seek for rest,
to labor and to look for no reward,
except that of knowing that I do your holy will. Amen.

—*Ignatius of Loyola*

49

I will go to the altar of God.
It is not myself and my tiny little affairs that matter here,
but the great sacrifice of atonement.
I surrender myself entirely to your divine will, O Lord.
Make my heart grow greater and wider,
out of itself, into the Divine Life.

—*Edith Stein*

50

Lord, I do not know what I ought to be asking of you.
You are the only One who knows what I need.
You love me better than I know how to love myself.
O Father!—give your child what I do not know how to
ask for myself.
I do not dare ask for crosses or consolation.
All I can do is present myself to you.
Lord, I open up my heart to you.
Behold my needs—the ones that I am not even aware of.
Look at them, and act according to your mercy.
Bring suffering on me or heal me, cast me down or raise me
   up—
I adore your will for me even when I do not know what it is.
I will remain silent,
offering myself up and giving myself over completely to you.
I no longer have any desire other than to accomplish your
   will.
Teach me to pray;
may you yourself pray in me and through me.

—*François Fénelon*

51

O merciful God, grant me grace,
fervently to desire all that is pleasing to you,
to examine it prudently,
to acknowledge it truthfully,
and to accomplish it perfectly,
for the praise and glory of your name.

—*Thomas Aquinas*

Suffering

52

Let the disorder in my body
be the means through which my soul is put into order.
I can now find no happiness in physical things;
let me find happiness only in you.

—*Blaise Pascal*

53

Dear Lord,
if this is how you treat your friends,
it is no wonder you have so few.

—*Teresa of Avila*

54

O my God, I thank you and I praise
you for accomplishing your holy
and all-lovable will without any regard for mine.
With my whole heart,
in spite of my heart,
do I receive this cross I feared so much!

It is the cross of your choice,
the cross of your love.
I venerate it;
nor for anything in the world
would I wish that it had not come,
since you willed it.

I keep it with gratitude and with joy,
as I do everything that comes from your hand;
and I shall strive to carry it without letting it drag,
with all the respect
and all the affection which your works deserve.

—*Francis de Sales*

55

Lord, it seems you have taken away
all the blessings that I once had from you.
In your grace, please give me now
that one gift which every dog
seems to have by nature—
that of being faithful to you in my distress,
faithful even when all comfort is gone.
This I desire more passionately
than anything else there is.
Amen.

—Mechthild of Magdeburg

56

When the signs of age begin to mark my body
(and still more when they touch my mind);
when the ill that is to diminish me or carry me off
strikes from without or is born within me;
When the painful moment comes
in which I suddenly awaken
to the fact that I am ill or growing old;
and above all at that last moment
when I feel I am losing hold of myself
and am absolutely passive within the hands
of the great unknown forces that have formed me;
in all these dark moments, O God,
grant that I may understand that it is you
(provided my faith is strong enough)
who are painfully parting the fibers of my being
in order to penetrate to the very marrow
of my substance and bear me away within yourself.

—*Pierre Teilhard de Chardin*

57

O Lord Christ, who in this difficult world
was tempted in all things, as I am,
yet fell into no sin,
look pitifully, I pray you, upon me.
Guide me with your adorable wisdom.
Teach me in everything and in every hour what I ought to do.
You alone know both that I suffer and what I need.
To you, that perfect path that I should walk is known.
Show it to me and teach me how to walk it.
Keep me, O Savior, in body, mind, and spirit,
for into your strong and gentle hands I commit myself.

—*Evelyn Underhill*

Union
with God

58

Jesus, my feet are dirty.
Come even as a slave to me,
pour water into your bowl,
come and wash my feet.
In asking such a thing I know I am overbold,
but I dread what was threatened when you said to me,
"If I do not wash your feet I have no fellowship
with you."
Wash my feet then,
because I long for your
companionship.

—*Origen*

59

Lord, you are my lover,
my longing,
my flowing stream,
my sun,
and I am your reflection.

—*Mechthild of Magdeburg*

60

O God my Truth,
make me one with you in eternal love.
Often I become weary with reading and hearing many
    things.
You are all I want and desire.
Let all teachers be mute and creation keep silence before
    you.
Speak to me, you, and you alone.

—*Thomas à Kempis*

61

Come now, slight mortal,

turn aside, for a little while, from your daily affairs;

hide yourself for a time, from your disturbing thoughts.

Cast aside your burdensome cares,

and put away your toilsome business.

Make room for a little time with God;

and rest awhile in him.

Enter the inner chamber of your soul;

shut out all thoughts except those of God,

and those things that can help you find him;

close the door and look to him.

Speak now, my heart; speak now to God and say:

"I seek your face;

it is your face, Lord, that I seek" (Psalm 27:8).

Come to me, now, O Lord my God,

teach my heart where and how it may seek you,

where and how it may find you.

—Anselm of Canterbury

62

O give yourself to me,
for without you no gift at all can satisfy.
And because you yourself are the gift,
O give me what you are,
that I may give you what I am,
and be made a partaker of the divine nature.

—*Thomas Traherne*

63

Pitch your tent within me,
gracious Master;
take up your dwelling in me now
and remain in your servant unceasingly,
inseparably,
to the end.

—*Simeon the New Theologian*

64

Thought is no longer of worth to me,
Nor work, nor speech.
Love draws me so high
(Thought is no longer of worth to me)
With her divine gaze,
That I have no intent.
Thought is no longer of worth to me,
Nor work, nor speech.

—*Marguerite Porete*

65

Lord, enfold me in the depths of your heart;
and there hold me,
refine, purge,
and set me on fire,
raise me aloft,
until my own self knows utter annihilation.

—*Pierre Teilhard de Chardin*

66

Lord, I will seek your face

and continually search for your face

as much as I can and as much as you render me capable of
doing.

Lord, my God, my one hope,

hear me lest exhausted I lose the will to seek you.

May I ardently seek you always.

Give the strength to seek, you who have given the desire.

And when the strength is sufficient,

add to the desire that which you have given.

May I always remember you, understand you, and love you
until,

faithfully remembering you,

prudently understanding you,

and truthfully loving you,

O Triune God,

according to the fullness which you know,

you reform me to your image in which you have created me.

—*William of St-Thierry*

Essential Mystic Prayers

67

I am as certain as I live that nothing is as close to me as
    God.
God is nearer to me than I am to my own self.
My life depends on God's being near to me,
present in me.

—*Meister Eckhart*

68

The Our Father contains all possible petitions;
we cannot conceive of any prayer not already contained in
    it.
It is to prayer what Christ is to humanity.
It is impossible to say it once through,
giving the fullest possible attention to each word,
without a change, infinitesimal perhaps but real,
taking place in the soul.

—*Simone Weil*

69

Where are you pasturing your flock, O good Shepherd,
who carry the whole flock on your shoulders?
For the whole of human nature is one sheep
and you have lifted it onto your shoulders.
Show me the place of peace,
lead me to the good grass that will nourish me,
call me by name so that I, your sheep, hear your voice,
and by your speech give me eternal life.
Answer me, you whom my soul loves.

—*Gregory of Nyssa*

70

Jesus, I love you.

—*Kateri Tekakwitha*

71

Batter my heart, three-person'd God; for, you
As yet but knock, breathe, shine, and seek to mend;
That I may rise, and stand, o'erthrow me, and bend
Your force, to break, blow, burn, and make me new.

—*John Donne*

72

Deepen your love in me, O Lord,

that I may learn in my inmost heart how sweet it is to love,
to be dissolved,

and to plunge myself into your love.

Let your love possess and raise me above myself,

with a fervor and wonder beyond imagination.

Let me sing the song of love.

Let me follow you into the heights.

Let my soul spend itself in your praise, rejoicing for love.

Let me love you more than myself, and myself only for your
      sake.

Let me love others, as your law commands.

—*Thérèse of Lisieux*

Essential Mystic Prayers

73

O Truth who is eternity:
Love who is Truth,
Eternity who is Love.
You are my God:
how could I not long for you
day and night.

—Augustine of Hippo

74

The lover of silence draws close to God.
He talks to God in secret and
God enlightens him.

—John Climacus

75

God, of your goodness, give yourself to me;
for you are enough for me,
and I can ask for nothing less than what fully honors you.
And if I do ask anything less,
then I will always be in want,
for only in you do I have everything.

—*Julian of Norwich*

76

This is our wisest and our best desire,
to be a splendid lover to our Most Glorious God.

—*Lilian Stavely*

77

"God is love. Whoever lives in love lives in God, and God
        in him."
May all of us attain this love of which I speak.
So help us, our Lord Jesus Christ. Amen.

—*Meister Eckhart*

Essential Mystic Prayers

Holy Presence

78

Gracious and Holy Father,
Please give me:
intellect to understand you,
reason to discern you,
diligence to seek you,
wisdom to find you,
a spirit to know you,
a heart to meditate upon you,
ears to hear you,
eyes to to see you,
a tongue to proclaim you,
a way of life pleasing to you,
patience to wait for you
and perseverance to look for you.
Grant me a perfect end,
your holy presence,
a blessed resurrection
and life everlasting.

—*Benedict of Nursia*

79

Fire of the Spirit, life of the lives of creatures,
spiral of sanctity, bond of all natures,
glow of charity, lights of clarity,
taste of sweetness to sinners—
be with us and hear us.

Composer of all things, light of all the risen,
key of salvation, release from the dark prison,
hope of all unions, scope of all chastities,
joy in the glory, strong honor—
be with us and hear us.

—*Hildegard of Bingen*

Essential Mystic Prayers

80

Who are you, sweet Light, that fills me,
And illumines the darkness of my heart?
You lead me like a mother's hand,
And should you let go of me,
I would not know how to take another step.
You are the space
That embraces my being and buries it in yourself.
Away from you it sinks into the abyss
Of nothingness, from which you raised it to the light.
You, nearer to me than I to myself
And more interior than my most interior,
And still impalpable and intangible
And beyond any name;
Holy Spirit, eternal love!

—*Edith Stein*

81

Whoever loves true prayer
and yet becomes angry or resentful
is his own enemy.
He is like a man who wants to see clearly
and yet inflicts damage on his own eyes.

—*Evagrius of Pontus*

82

Lord, help me to do great things as though they were little,
since I do them with your power;
and little things as though they were great,
since I do them in your name.

—*Blaise Pascal*

83

Be kind to your little children, Lord.

Be a gentle teacher, patient with our weakness and stupidity.

And give us the strength and discernment to do what you
    tell us,

and so grow in your likeness.

May we all live in the peace that comes from you.

May we journey toward your city,

sailing through the waters of sin untouched by the waves,

borne serenely along by the Holy Spirit.

Night and day may we give you praise and thanks,

because you have shown us that all things belong to you,

and all blessings are gifts from you.

To you, the essence of wisdom, the foundation of truth,

be glory for evermore.

—*Clement of Alexandria*

84

Fortify me with the grace of your Holy Spirit
and give your peace to my soul
that I may be free from all needless anxiety, solicitude, and
      worry.
Help me to desire always that which is pleasing and
      acceptable to you
so that your Will may be my will.
Grant that I may rid myself of all unholy desires
and that, for your love,
I may remain obscure and unknown in this world,
to be known only to you.
Do not permit me to attribute to myself
the good that you perform in me and through me,
but rather, referring all honor to your Majesty,
may I glory only in my infirmities,
so that renouncing sincerely all vainglory which comes from
      the world,
I may aspire to that true and lasting glory which comes from
      you. Amen.

—*Mother Cabrini*

85

O my God, teach my heart where and how to seek you,
where and how to find you....
You are my God and you are my All and I have never seen
you.
You have made me and remade me,
You have bestowed on me all the good things I possess,
Still I do not know you....
I have not yet done that for which I was made....
Teach me to seek you....
I cannot seek you unless you teach me
or find you unless you show yourself to me.
Let me seek you in my desire, let me desire you in my
seeking.
Let me find you by loving you, let me love you when I find
you.

—*Anselm of Canterbury*

86

I ask you neither for health nor for sickness, for life nor for
      death;

but that you may dispose of my health and my sickness, my
      life

and my death, for your glory.

You alone know what is expedient for me; you are the
      sovereign master;

do with me according to your will.

Give to me, or take away from me, only conform my will to
      yours.

I know but one thing, Lord, that it is good to follow you, and
      bad to offend you.

Apart from that, I know not what is good or bad in anything.

I know not which is most profitable for me, health or
      sickness,

wealth or poverty, nor anything else in the world.

That discernment is beyond the power of men or angels, and
      is hidden

among the secrets of your Providence, which I adore, but do
      not seek to fathom.

—*Blaise Pascal*

87

May Jesus enter into us
and clear out
and cast away all hindrances of soul and body,
to the end that we may be one with him here upon earth
and there in heaven.
So help us, God. Amen.

—*Meister Eckhart*

88

O Lord, fill my heart with eternal life.

—*Isaac the Syrian*

The Authors of These Prayers

Anselm of Canterbury (1033–1109). Monk, abbot, and for twenty years Archbishop of Canterbury, Anselm is remembered for his writings on the Incarnation and for his succinct definition of theology as "faith seeking understanding."

Augustine of Hippo (354–430). His influence, particularly on the Western church, cannot be overestimated. His *Confessions*, a personal account of his life and conversion, remains an enduring testament to the work of God in a human soul.

Bede the Venerable (c. 670–735) was only seven when his family gave him to the monastery. He became a prominent scholar and beloved teacher, remembered by his students not only for his knowledge, but for his deep devotion to the monastic life.

Benedict of Nursia (c. 480–c. 550) is known as the founder of Western monasticism, and the patron saint of Europe and all monks.

Bernard of Clairvaux (1090–1153). Known for his skills as a preacher and theologian, Bernard was a leader of reform within the Benedictine life of his time. He emphasized the place of mystical prayer within the context of ordinary monastic observance.

Blaise Pascal (1623–1662) was a French mathematician and physicist, who nevertheless recognized the limits of reason when it comes to matters of faith. His own mystical experiences led him to pronounce that "the heart has its reasons which reason does not know at all."

Brother Lawrence (c. 1614–1691). Nicolas Herman, who became known as Brother Lawrence of the Resurrection, was a Carmelite lay brother and a mystic. His life of almost constant recollection was lived largely through his work in the kitchen of his monastery, where he practiced the presence of God in all things.

C. S. Lewis (1893–1963) was a scholar and Christian apologist. His conversion to Christianity is recorded in his spiritual autobiography, *Surprised by Joy*. His writings have had a profound influence, including his beloved *Chronicles of Narnia*.

Catherine of Siena (1347–1380) was born the second youngest of twenty-five children. She became a third-order Dominican at a very early age. Even while devoting herself to the care of the poor and sick of her plague-infested city, Catherine embraced a life of contemplative prayer and mystical experience.

Clement of Alexandria (c. 140–c. 220) presents the Christian life as a spiritual journey in which the soul, by the work of the Holy Spirit, is gradually "deified," becoming more and more united with God.

Dimitrii of Rostov (1651–1709), a monk and ascetic, was a devoted researcher who spent twenty years compiling a record of Russian saints. He composed hymns and other musical works, but was best known for his devotion to prayer. On the day of his death, he was discovered on his knees before an icon of Christ the Savior.

Edith Stein (1891–1942), a philosopher and a convert to Roman Catholicism, Stein became a Carmelite nun, Teresa Benedicta of the Cross. To escape arrest by the Nazis, she fled from Germany to the Netherlands, where she was eventually found, imprisoned, and put to death in the gas chambers of Auschwitz.

Ephrem the Syrian (c. 306–373) is considered the greatest poet of the early Christian centuries. Described by some of his contemporaries as the "Harp of the Spirit," he was known as well for his prayerful and ascetic life. He died in Edessa ministering to victims of the plague.

Evagrius of Pontus (346–399) became a noted preacher in Constantinople. A vocation to monastic life led him to the Egyptian desert, where he became the first monk to write extensively on the spiritual life. He brought deep psychological insight to his works on prayer, contemplation, sin, and spiritual growth.

Evelyn Underhill (1875–1941) is the author of a much-loved classic, *Mysticism*. She was an English poet, novelist, artist, and much sought after spiritual counselor and retreat leader. Much of the focus in her later years was on the work of the Holy Spirit.

Francis de Sales (1567–1622) was the author of the classic work *Introduction to the Devout Life*. There he wrote that the way of spiritual perfection is not limited to an elite few, nor does it require a life of severe austerity. Without extreme withdrawal from everyday life, the Christian may still pursue a life of deep devotion and prayer.

Francis of Assisi (1181–1226), one of the most popular saints of the church and founder of the Franciscan Order, is known for his passionate devotion to Christ and his love of the poor.

François Fénelon (1651–1715) was a French archbishop who became a counselor to members of the court of Louis XIV. Though political intrigues led to a time of exile, he continued his spiritual work and his efforts on behalf of the poor in his diocese. The influence of his letters and spiritual meditations continues today.

George Herbert (1593–1633) was ordained a vicar and became associated with a small religious community in Little Gidding. From there he went on to work as both a pastor and a poet. His hymns are still popular, and his poetry has earned him a leading place in English literature.

Gerard Manley Hopkins (1844–1899) was a Jesuit priest and professor of Greek in Dublin. Received into the Catholic Church by John Henry Newman, Hopkins brought a love of art, a deep study of the classics, and a fresh approach to poetry.

Gregory of Nyssa (c. 330–394), the third of the three so-called Cappadocian Fathers (together with Basil and Gregory Nazianzus), became known for his spiritual writings and his promotion of the monastic life. He argued that the Christian pursued God not as an object to be understood, but as a mystery to be loved.

Hildegard of Bingen (1098–1179) is known to have undergone various supernatural experiences, and particularly visions, which she recorded, about the heavenly life, creation, and the meaning of salvation. From the age of eight she was raised in a Benedictine environment and eventually became an abbess.

Ignatius of Loyola (1491–1556), founder of the Society of Jesus (the Jesuits), underwent a conversion that was influenced by the life of Christ and the lives of the saints. Many of his insights into the Christian life are reflected in the *Spiritual Exercises*, one of the classics of Western spirituality.

Isaac the Syrian (died c. 700), also known as Isaac of Nineveh, as a young man became a monk, and only months after his consecration as a bishop fled to the mountains to live out his life in solitude. His influence was spread particularly through his *Ascetical Treatises*.

Jean-Pierre de Caussade (1675–1751) became a Jesuit and was soon recognized as an effective preacher, spiritual director, and defender of mysticism. He carried out an extensive correspondence with the Sisters of the Visitation, and it is largely from those writings that his *Abandonment to Divine Providence* was produced.

John Climacus (c. 570 c. 649) was a monk of the monastery of Mount Sinai, now St. Catherine's Monastery. After living in community, he took up life as a hermit and wrote the work for which he is named, *The Ladder of Paradise*, in which he presents thirty "steps" (one for each year of Jesus's life before his baptism) for pursuing the spiritual life.

John Donne (1571–1631) was ordained an Anglican priest and became Dean of St. Paul's Cathedral in London. He was known for his preaching, in which he placed great emphasis on the mercy of God. His religious poetry became recognized for its dramatic style and its deep expression of love for and union with God.

John Henry Newman (1801–1890), brought up in the Church of England and ordained a priest, carried out a fruitful career as a preacher and writer. But from his Evangelical roots he gradually developed a more Catholic view of the church. In 1845, he was received as a Roman Catholic and became a cardinal.

John of the Cross (1542–1591), the son of a poor but noble family in Spain, entered a Carmelite monastery as a teenager. He was ordained a priest and soon after met Teresa of Avila, with whom he worked for the reform of the Carmelite Order. His poetry and mystical writings speak with rich imagery of the heart's pursuit of God.

Joyce Rupp, OSM (1943–), a member of the Servants of Mary, is a writer, retreat leader, conference speaker, and author of a number of best-selling books. She is the co-director of the Institute for Compassionate Presence and an active volunteer for hospice.

Julian of Norwich (c. 1342–c. 1420) lived a life of solitude as an anchoress in a cell attached to the church of St. Edmund and St. Julian in Norwich, England. She experienced a series of visions that revealed aspects of the love of God, the passion of Christ, and the Trinity. Her meditations are contained in *Revelations of Divine Love*, the first book written in English by a woman.

Kateri Tekakwitha (1656–1680), the first Native American to have been beatified in the Catholic Church, was orphaned at four when she and her entire family contracted smallpox. She met Christian missionaries in 1667, and was baptized on Easter Sunday, 1676. She spent the remainder of her short life devoted to prayer, fasting, teaching children, and caring for the sick and aged.

Lilian Staveley (1878–1928) kept her spiritual life a secret to those closest to her, even her husband. In three anonymously written books, *The Prodigal Returns, The Romance of the Soul,* and *The Golden Fountain,* she describes how a Christian may live an inner life of mystical converse with God in combination with an outward life of ordinary activity.

Madame Guyon (1648–1717) was controversial in her time (she was accused of heresy and even imprisoned), but today is recognized for her mystical experiences in prayer and her teaching on complete detachment from the world for the sake of loving God. Her prayer of simplicity and silence is echoed by Quakers and other Pietistic traditions.

Margery Kempe (c. 1373–after 1438). Nearly everything known of her comes from her own work, *The Book of Margery Kempe,* in which she describes her multiple pilgrimages and mystical experiences. Despite accusations of heresy, Kempe successfully defended her orthodox faith, and her writing has enjoyed renewed interest in recent generations.

Marguerite Porete (1250–1310), author of *The Mirror of Simple Souls,* was burned at the stake in Paris for continuing to circulate copies of the book after it was declared heretical. She has been compared with Mechthild of Magdeburg (see below) for emphasizing freedom in the Spirit and the mystical qualities of divine love, a common theme of the Beguine movement (medieval women who lived intensely pious, though non-monastic lives).

Mechthild of Magdeburg (c. 1210–1280), author of a book of mystical revelations, began to experience visions of the love of God from the age of twelve. She became a Beguine under the spiritual direction of Dominicans in Magdeburg and, after forty years, was professed as a nun in the Cistercian convent of Helfta, where she completed her writings.

Meister Eckhart (c. 1260–c. 1328) was a German Dominican theologian and preacher. He wrote of the soul's intimate union with God, which is the true source of the Christian life. Despite accusations of heresy, his writings continued to be studied and copied in and beyond the Dominican Order.

Mother Cabrini (1850–1917), or Frances Xavier Cabrini, was the first US citizen to be canonized by the Catholic Church. In 1887, she founded the Missionary Sisters of the Sacred Heart, especially dedicated to the service of Italian immigrants in America and elsewhere.

Nicholas of Cusa (1401–1464) was a cardinal, philosopher, astronomer, and reformer of the church. Together with his many recorded sermons, theological writings, and scientific studies, his mystical writings have made him one of the most important German thinkers of the fifteenth century.

Origen (c. 185–c. 254), arguably the leading mind of early Christianity, was born in Egypt where he became the leading representative of the Alexandrian school of theology. He was a biblical scholar, but with a strong current of mysticism that is especially evident in his ascetical works, *On Prayer* and *An Exhortation to Martyrdom*.

Patrick of Ireland (mid- or late fifth century) is one of the most legendary and popular figures in Christianity. Born in Britain and held prisoner for a time in Ireland, he eventually returned to his place of captivity to evangelize, establish churches, and found monasteries.

Pierre Teilhard de Chardin (1881–1955) was a Jesuit theologian and scientist who sought to bring the Christian tradition into harmony with contemporary scientific understandings about nature and creation. For him, all matter has a sacramental character, rooted in the Incarnation and moving toward fulfillment in God.

Simone Weil (1909–1943) was a French philosopher and activist for the Resistance in World War II. Raised in a Jewish, agnostic home, she nevertheless felt a profound attraction to Christianity. She records in her spiritual autobiography, *Waiting on God*, that one of her most profound religious experiences took place in the Basilica of St. Mary of the Angels, the same church in Assisi where Francis prayed.

Simeon the New Theologian (949–1022). After an early career of imperial service in Constantinople, Simeon entered monastic life and became an abbot. His greatest contribution, however, was as a mystic and spiritual writer, combining both the private contemplative tradition with an emphasis on the importance of community life.

Teresa of Avila (1515–1582), together with John of the Cross, is known for her work in reforming the Carmelite Order, resulting in the founding of the Discalced Carmelites. Just as important, however, was her contribution to the spiritual life, especially represented by her account of mystical experience in *The Interior Castle*.

Thérèse of Lisieux (1873–1897). Drawn to religious life from an early age, Thérèse joined a Carmelite monastery at fifteen. Her simple and practical approach to the spiritual life is reflected in her autobiography, *The Story of a Soul*, which she wrote at the direction of her superiors.

Thomas à Kempis (c. 1380–1471) was educated by the Brethren of the Common Life, an association of clergy and laity dedicated to a high level of Christian devotion and practice. He gave himself to work as a preacher, spiritual director, and writer. His classic work, *The Imitation of Christ*, has been translated into more languages than any other book apart from the Bible.

Thomas Aquinas (c. 1225–1274) was a Dominican philosopher and theologian. He is one of the most influential figures in the history of the Christian church. Though his most famous work is the *Summa Theologiae* (Latin "Synthesis of Theology"), he is equally known as a man of deep devotion and prayer.

Thomas Merton (1915–1968). While a student at Columbia University, Merton converted to Catholicism and in 1944 entered the Trappist Abbey of Gethsemani in Kentucky. Among his prolific writings, his autobiography, *The Seven Storey Mountain*, inspired countless numbers of his generation to explore the spirituality of monastic life.

Thomas Traherne (c. 1636–1674). After studying at Oxford, Traherne was ordained and served as both a parish priest and private chaplain. His poems, for which he is now famous, were not published until 1903. In them, he concentrates on the glory of creation, and of childhood, with little to no reference to sin or suffering.

William of St-Thierry (c. 1085–1148) entered a Benedictine monastery, where he spent twenty years as a monk before being elected abbot of St-Thierry. After meeting Bernard of Clairvaux, with whom he shared a close friendship, he resigned his abbacy and joined a small group of Cistercian monks to establish a new monastery. Drawn to theological study and contemplative prayer, William wrote extensively about the spiritual life.

Essential Mystic Prayers